The Lost Notebook

Jennie Feldman

The Lost Notebook

ANVIL PRESS POETRY

Published in 2005
by Anvil Press Poetry Ltd
Neptune House 70 Royal Hill London SE10 8RF
www.anvilpresspoetry.com

This book is published with financial assistance
from Arts Council England

Designed and set in Monotype Ehrhardt by Anvil
Printed at Alden Press Limited
Oxford and Northampton

ISBN 0 85646 381 7

A catalogue record for this book
is available from the British Library

for Phil
and for my mother

ACKNOWLEDGEMENTS

Some of the poems in this collection, or earlier versions of them, have appeared in *London Magazine*, *Metre*, *Parnassus*, *PN Review*, *The Jerusalem Review*, *Thumbscrew*.

CONTENTS

SEA DAFFODILS

Because the book that has your photo
says you'll die tomorrow, here I am
hooked on your single day's extravagance.
For this is the way we ride the dune,
bareback with tilted trumpets, lost for music
and knowing we'll never hear it again
that pale arpeggio of geese pulling south
to one long note diminuendo. Because
there's broken glass left and right, and ants
are heading my way over the sand,
I lean into your cool white space and breathe
a faint kindness. So it is, once again,
the immensity of existing things
rooted here in an exclamation,
six girlish sepals leaning back to laugh.
There's hardly time to understand
the hilarity; already yesterday's has trailed off
to meet its shadow. And something irrepressible
is bulging at the base of withered stems,
the risqué joke I'll never get
though no doubt it's to do with tiny headstones
thrusting through your bleached sprawl of leaves.
Busy being born, busy dying,
fugitive perfection on a barren shore, you
wrench from the guts an answering cry,
autumn, autumn, autumn.

BONFIRE ON THE BEACH

Tragedy was short-lived:
where the pine log had split its sides

dying, a spider elbowed out
and flared a brief nothing.

Old as planets the four faces
round this sun. A smudge

on the sand, like a mistake,
will mean we've gone.

A FIFTH STRING

Scuttling crabwise all elbows and knees
– a dancer's inspired deformity? –
she waves a wild hello with outsize
pincers, and a man in grinning close-up
thrums a hairbrush banjo-style,
even though it's over
and I'm waking

to a ship's colossal blare across the bay –
stunning the air, humming
in the bones with certainty
like a tuning-fork struck into song.
Behind closed lids I hear it, fathoms down,
that sunken A a bass might reach
on some fifth string.

And I wish the sea had kept to itself
the evening catch hauled up through livid silk.
All those sardine eyes seeing everything and
nothing for the first time. Perfect mouths
open, shut, losing the beat, miming
deadpan a music-hall number, its tender
absurdities.

CHROMATIC

Was it for the music? – Manic
chords smashing on the downbeat
to a heap of glass. You'd have to stand
here, knee-deep in sea lavender
a dozen paces from the ruined wall:
close enough to aim and hit
the mark, but out of splinters' reach.
Or perhaps the provocation –
all those bottles dead smooth
as if drunk was it, and it
never enough. Again and again
right on target till the green
and brown glitter rises sharp
as sacrifice. Shrieks in the small hours,
wild limbs. No telling.
Now morning's sober consequence plays
light across the dunes where the old notations
– rodent tread, lizard squiggle – hold.
Regarding such things, and startling
accidentals that do and don't belong,
a syringe half-buried in sand.
Wondering what that stranger
at the water's edge watching me
means. Which music he's picking up.
Which of us this generous space
will swallow in one swig mid-phrase
not missing a beat.

MERIDIAN

I

Out there on the far rock's last fling
a profiled figure from whose groin
slant, slender rapture three times
his length lifts unreeling
against the horizon. *Euoi!*
I shall take to the hills
crowned with ivy, fawn skin
straining the safety pins
as I dance by torchlight to flutes
and tympanon.

II

Hauled from Pygmalion's bed, gently,
not to jolt a dream's buffed ivory

or muss the chiselled hair already
yielding to the sea wind, she stands.

And two skinny youths, their solemn hands
idolatrous with sunscreen for her back.

Astonished space. Save. Cut and paste
votively here.

OGYGIA

Calypso

Not so much love as the careless act
of shipwreck, I suspect, each night
you're washed ashore. Cinemascope
on your mind's far wall and me

in the dark. O singular man, this distance

of yours. The sea's vast habit singing
in your blood, so that even asleep
when your limbs' encircling longitude, latitude
pin me down, I'm not the point.

Take the measure, they said, of his longing.

Deploy the slow unbraiding of your hair.
Spin it out. Seal your name in each
soft hollow. – As if I believed the fantasy.
As if I dared to hope the poem ends here.

Odysseus

Sometimes I could swear it's the other
voice murmuring long-distance in my ear.
But the shape you take in the dark
is yours, these hands having long since lost
all memory of home ... Then the crunch
come morning and shells' dead glory
underfoot. *Immortality?* But I'm dying
of this protracted present tense, the sea's
unbearable sameness without me.
These nights that hang an anchor-stone
smooth around my neck – till I'm thrashing
for air, clinging fast, washed up sprawling
in the surf, again, as the static hiss
all but drowns *Odysseus, Odysseus ...*

FLYING FISH

Yoannis was there. Saw the two black devils
smirking in the storm-plucked rigging above their heads.
So he once confided. Against such things he wears
a sprig of wild mint tucked behind one ear
and a Byzantine innocence salvaged
from that boat pitched head-high on the wall;
the chapel his last stop before the village,
though whether to pray or just drop in
on old companions in trouble, hard to say.
No family of his own. Unless you count
the whimpering bundle of rags two walkers found
abandoned at a road's end in the hills.
An aunt of his, it's said. Yoannis squints
against the sea glare. Talks to himself,
the words mysterious and only their rhythms
visible in the cigarette that jives
against his beard. But that hardly explains
why he leapt to mind one morning
when streaks of silver suddenly arched
right out of the water, converting everything.

PENINSULA

All night a scatty murmur
from the corner where the small fridge
occasionally shudders; the sense
of concertina'd rocks whose silence
the sea is playing on. To step out

of one's skin and feel the sirocco
breathing tender landfall,
how the stars' domed arrangement
fits the moment's gravity
in the small hours. And I think

of the octopus Stavros caught
and diced to a glittering constellation
above unworldly fish. By morning
they'll lie agog on ice, *the image
as a caricature of being.*

Already the air thinning
to a mild hope of dawn. Just time
to fetch an offering of grapes
olives and kefalotiri cheese
before definition sets in.

GORGE

Black Eyes, beloved of Nikolas,
how long can we
go on munching
black pods
in a carob's wry shade?
        There's green
            leaning
sweetly on air
        down there
    where daredevil clefts
        pocket the dew.
                Black Eyes
beloved of Nikolas,
       high horned
     against the sky, pressed
      to the likeness
of *kri-kri* imprinted on clay
           how these ruminations
           waggle your
           stern goatee.
               Let's agree,
if one of us slips
and it's you
    I'll zigzag down
to put out your slotted gaze
   take off
   your gold-plated bell
   for Nikolas

and if it's me
    you'll make a meal
                        of this page.
Yassu, Black Eyes!
    Dainty-
            footed over the
edge we
        go.

PLATEAU

No longer beautiful the two old birds
shelved and cock-eyed, keeping up a show
of pheasant plumage. It could be theirs,
the meek arthritic flutter bringing
métrio coffee outside where
it trembles in the suddenness of sky.

What can break a plateau's stone gaze?
Olive trees exchange long silences
about the cold that took their fruit;
a wild pear's profusion goes begging.
And absence hums to itself, shrugging
off roofs, doors, masonry in scruffy fields.

She didn't say: I have known love, small cries
softer than the sea's undoing. Nor
All I have is the moment of my life.
But when she quickened at my greeting
on the road, one clawed hand lifted mutely
to her heart, and beat time twice on her breast.

HOLD

Spiked on rocks, still it plays the ark
– the rage that flung it high and dry

a miracle, startling the sceptic
whose habit combs every shore
for clues. It balances, razor shell
still hinged to cup a purpose, a ghost

or whoever having found the gash
climbs inside, moves through *The Plassey*'s
freight of rusted shadow, and sky
a small icon overhead where white

ribbon weeds grip and hang as long
as it takes. Hard to say how long
it took – lost among buckled struts
rivets unbuttoned by the floor's heave –

to recognize the foreign calm
for what it was, neither here nor there
but capsuled in thin air between
the grim burlesque of men roping

ashore through surf, and solitude content
to be the sum of its subtractions.

BLUE

Now there's no holding them back,
all the fictions that doggedly
tag along in hope of a moment

like this where the dunes' falling cadence
brings on the sea. So that almost
anything, even the far-fetched

sighting on the tip of the tongue,
goes. And the battered pair of boots
that got here first, sand in the creases

resumes a gentle soliloquy,
paces out the *Tristia* in rhythms
of cerulean blue. It comes to this,

listening for sounds that exile makes
– beyond the surf's drumrolled punchline –
the perfect pitch of something

loved and lost. Which is why we're
back for the umpteenth time. Primed
for ultramarine, blazoned with it

when we leave, as kingfishers keep
the wingflash even in dry savannas
swooping for mites, and only a cobalt streak

to recall the deeper plunge.

All morning
a famished, familiar suspense,
and on my lips the salt taste of waves.

EAST WIND

And then there's a sadness not even
uproarious sea can budge or fudge
into purple confection. Abstract nouns
too heavy. No point, either, combing a shore
for quirks if the crows have got there first,
one strutting off with a matchbox stupid
in its beak, another ripping the blob
a jellyfish was. Bright-eyed the day
denies longing. Not to turn and wade
in deep, just tread sky-dazzle along the rim,
tightrope the continuum ...
                              So what now?
Now what, what now?
                        O tell about
the waves' fine spray flung backflip
pulling my gaze slap slap it's a sail
being lowered in the squall of off-beat
counterwheeling gulls that bring in the crows
two octaves lower – spare and hoarse and cool
altogether – as a sweep of dimples
gladdens the bay and a tumbleweed ball
skipping away over breakers rolls
light and lonely out to sea.

THE LOST NOTEBOOK

Back then into the surf's commotion
(*where the sea moves the word moves ...*)
under the sway of water as fish
with barcodes on their tails
fan the sand's ribbing.
It's a start.
Tot up the losses, time
in tier upon tier of breakers.
– Facing that long roar
as it swells beyond all measure
to pound head-over-heels
sforzando, the cry lifts like a sob,
the conductor in shirtsleeves pleading:
Con gioia! Con gioia!
because the *Pastoral* can't contain itself.
Like that day the floortiles heaved and growled
and crockery rattled in the thrill of it.
Or first-time murmurings at which
the eucalyptus fingered sky more frantically
than ever. So now they're out,
thoughts that drummed a gallop
in the mind. Take a stick, smooth
the churned sand and write:

    Whose voice, this moody
    subjunctive (doubt, desire) slant
    on a salt-edged wind?

A dog with a hind leg missing sniffs
between the syllables. Briefly

the stump quivers. Then he's off, grinning
and waltzing along the frilly shore.
Bidart's one-armed man
tried to convince himself
The lost arm had never existed
and failed. It's an art –
remembering to forget, or vice versa.
Carob trees have it. Entire limbs
casually drop off as if those years
didn't count. The tree no less a tree.
Sad delights we re-invent,
the scent of pines randomly
held in place by nothing, just birds
more song than body
in spaces nothing else can fill.
(Don't move, don't even blink –
there it is, sunning on a rock:
the word *never* pretends it too
is rock, its furtive pulsing
just under the ribs a shameless fantasy
between your stepping closer and the quick
flick of its vanishing.) How to hold on
to the almost nothing. Over and over.
The owl's faltering certainty
on syllables of moon it has perfected.
Such things to worship. Or invite
into the quiet habitation of a book,
letting our words fall senseless
under noon leaves' figgy
exhalations. Melody drops
away and there you are
tympanist behind and above
everything, beating mad complicities

from the hollow beneath the skin,
damping with a swift palm whatever strays
beyond its bars. Oh I have
strayed.

        Beside me on the sand he said:
Memory is a fact of the soul
and he furrowed a four-finger stanza
for something to root in:

    A skirting of water
    round the prow
    of the headland
    – such voyages …

A little girl in an orange swimsuit
draws a bucketful, tips it over a smaller
unsuspecting child at the water's edge:
"What's your name?" Downcast silence.
So it begins, the one-sided game:
dousing and asking. But the world has stopped
and in its merciless fixity
the child behind the dripping curtain
of hair finds no words or sound,
bows her head. Remembrance
at the siren hour: vanished names.
I'm listening hard … *these silences*
in which things yield and seem
about to betray their ultimate secret.
Even the dunes are sprouting ears
cocked green at different angles
to catch the veering whisper
off the sea. To an audience
of rapt yellow faces, I say:

Evening Primrose. Politely they nod
as one does to a foreigner
who thinks he's making sense.
And they get on with what matters,
stamens and pistils superbly erect.
But it's the flagging, red-veined
crepey ones that bring me
to my knees; all resistance
flipped to the winds.

Perhaps the pages' quiet detachment
from their spiral binding has finally
scattered, *fly away home*, and they're gone,
lines familiar, it seemed, as the back of my hand
– where I'm watching a blood-bright ladybird
trundle battered, a bit unhinged, having
doubtfully charted the other side's criss-crossing
love, longevity, handsome strangers.
Bold mite, mute parody of a dice
that never falls on six but flaunts the chanciness
of life seen from above, *your house is on fire.*
Almost underfoot your brilliant friends
– a swarm blown off-course? – on stone pedestals
unmoving. And the mind dawns bare
as the sea's layered distance. This teeming
silence, to begin with, or end. Terror
of not knowing which, *and your children
all alone.*

Degrees of vanishing:
Hadrian rendered in marble, sketched for keeps
with those notes years back. What's left? A notion
of thighs' nonchalance, the fluted fall of a robe,

the boundless gaze. But details of, say, flowers
in the Tauros, or café talk in Paris – no trace.
And those fragments for a love poem – inaudible now
above its music (*dolce … sempre più … sempre più*).

UNTITLED

Words having failed, I keep company
with jackals yowling lean as midnight
from the wadi. Bully-headed crows
scavenge with me where storms have scribbled
all down the shore. Hunger, the old ache

for wild unfenced unlabelled things that come
uncalled like gods, or nameless cats treading
over the silence of rusted wire.
If you see this pale green fire in the dusk
I'm coaxing a murmur from driftwood.

THE WAY A FIRE

The way a fire talks in tongues
you'd think it god's gift to man

the way it needs watchful stones
to ring it, a hollow to lie in
and space above for the sparks'

homeward flight. With hope tensed
for every hiss and smoke-breath

silken round the limbs' damp curves,
you'd think a fire meant life, even
that life without fire is void;

the ash through my fingers warm
still with all the unread signals.

PHOENIX EGG

When you're gargled and sucked by the sea
a few million years then lifted off a beach

people get ideas. As if you could broadcast
from a foreign desk the kelpie legends

of Skye, the grace notes flecking Loch Coruisk
or moaning calls of guillemots. As if

cupped in the palm like a phoenix egg
some unthought-of thing might hatch

or the alchemy of curve, dusk mauve, unfathomed silence
precipitate just the right words on the page.

NO TREES ON SOUTH UIST

and nothing to anchor sky
heaving over eye-level

from the west. Nothing but
what's underfoot. Was dominion

ever this easy or lonely
thinks the stranger standing forked

and puny in the sea wind.
Out on the machair grasses

light shifts, nothing else matters.

WINDOW SEAT

At just over forty thousand feet
death is belly-up beside me
shimmying on folded wings, tranced
behind glass in exquisite absence
beyond which every distance pales.

I invite him somewhere over Greece
to play the immortal scarab, be
my amulet against the earthbound
(islands heaving their wrinkles on cue).
But pity and terror have folded his legs

mutely in triple supplication,
brittled the feelers to question-marks,
like one who's been caught in the act
of dying, or lost some cherished certainty.

CANAL GRANDE

Pompeo Molmenti, eminent historian
this is to tell you the water now reaches
your third step. Your stone walls shudder
in green as I sit here, and two corks
a jellyfish and one half-opened rose signal
in passing the tide's coming in.
To be honest, step two is damp with fronds
where water-lice skid round my feet.
But at the timber door where you came
and went, your two lions still solemnize
our transience, one with a fine moustache, his paw
propped on a smaller beast whose ear he chews
or whispers into; the other balancing
between two poles, tail wrapped round his loins.
History as fable? A joke between friends?
Do you mind if your plaque captions this pair
with their shrinking flanks and eyes blinded
to bore-holes? Or that, with no dates to bracket
your life, I meet you adrift in time. Pompeo
Molmenti. Tell me the secret of buoyancy
when all one sees and belongs to is slowly
sinking. Somewhere between the skimming pose
of gondolas and limpet colonies' upward creep
how do you safeguard the honorable?
Our second step, Signor, is under water.

INTIFADA

he just lies there in my head as if
it used to be his, staring up at sky
or a ceiling long gone
                              I'm shaking
my head very slowly because
if he notices me, the enemy,
he'll never let me stroke his arm
or say I'm sorry he's dead

FIRST LIGHT

Still spinning out of night

blue held in skeins pale
enough to wrap a planet.

You could leap off this pier
whooping and be caught by the sheer
coherence of it all. One, two –

but any second now a wedge
of sail or some devout swimmer
will demarcate sea and sky, shore
and sea; navy gunships will come

cutting along the dotted line
to defend you.
              (And already
the vision is over, sandals rebuckled.
Light plays these tricks, briefly.)

DESERTER

A one-night stand, perhaps, but such
rousing from the mineral dead
can sweep you off your feet, rampant
waves from nowhere, their moonless pitch
monumentally desolate.
How many deaths can a dead sea die?
Thirst had never been an issue,
living with the salt itch, serenely.
But something cracks if what flows in
is strangled to a trickle. Cupped
in the desert a soul's parameters
start to shrink. Another few weeks
would have brought quick rains,
an ecstasy of wilderness flowers
but you couldn't wait. You tore
off your khaki shirt, seized your snare-
drum by the shoulder strap and running
to the water's edge flung it against
the sky, where it glints turning
over and over in my mind.

Dead Sea, 2003

MOTH

Hinged askew, two small wings fall

their silver stamped on my palm
and all purpose suddenly gone

both his and mine, that *idée fixe*
of sourcing the radiance of things

urgent now, with night in the air
and only this lamp, sixty watts

for a soft ghost circling in.

VETERAN

Tunnelling the dark, each breath
a bursting sigh to rise for

I have in mind hills innocent
as pebbles, low rocks that blink

into seals lazy on bladderwrack
and only the dainty explosion

of a sea-urchin dropped from high
unmourned, no shouts. Every thought

domed with that sky as I hunt
illegible squid deep into night

warm-blooded where other blood runs cold
and the slow sift of what used to float

islands me.
           No island lives alone
and mine must sometimes lie with yours

O Skye, listening to the sea break
its silence in soft expletives

before they come to refloat the bottle-
nose whale in Broadford Bay. Let's say

my barnacles gleamed like medals
the day they hauled me back and I sank.

ON TURNING OFF THE NEWS

With its vast memory the desert

recognizes me, takes me back
no questions asked. Which is why

I find myself from years ago coolly
floating between parched walls, a high

turquoise profile, rock and sky,
mirrored in the gorge of Wadi Zrara.

Dunes riffled by tidal winds (our tracks
won't last the day), and all the seething

mayhem hour by hour on the air
smothered to a stillness. Ochre, grey-pink

its crests and ridges fading to a shimmer,
Sinai is unfinished business

for moments like this. In its dry folds
even the smallest truth will keep

for centuries, like parchment or olive pits
or the stork we chanced on wide-winged

in some remembered flight.

HARMONIC

        One light
touch on a humming string flukes the note
unearthly high to vanish in distance;
the altered silence stays.

        Where sky
is mirrored square in the half-dozen fishponds,
a slow spiralling assembly shocks the eye
like revelation. Stretched necks and trailing legs
counterpoise wings that span five octaves
for thermals to play.

        Having perfect pitch
storks recognize the slightest modulation
that's when they arrow north.

IN TRANSLATION

for Jacques Réda

And now it's rained on your letter –
ink on the move giving words
the slip. Held to the light you
set the mind reeling. Again. *Jazziste*,
I think you'd like the way
phrases are coming through the page
in counterpoint from behind, leaning
back on the beat. How rhythm and sound
make sense. I'm listening, falling
into step with you in spring – clouds *furiously
slow* – as far as Place de la Bastille where
we clear a table for our languages
to meet, negotiate the finer points.
*Perhaps we should speak even more softly
So that silence can take refuge in our voices ...*
Then it comes through the stillness, something
like song sculling from your side to mine.

RENDEZ-VOUS

A friend is waving from the world's
far side. Any of these sailing-boats
for hire by the half-hour, decks
cleared ready, could take me.
But the steep V of a gull
alighting among them wrecks
all that: his beak's ironic curve
and the sweep of his stowed wings' upslant
ride the water comically higher
than the hulls. (*Méchant! Méchant!*
Children lunge with boating rods.)
I'm stranded, wobbling in his wake.

But in its pale disc his eye
knows the earth's spin backwards;
his silence all the oceans he's not telling
though I'd wait a lifetime.
Nothing but purpose, every move
streamlined to a ruthless chic.
Panic of desire as he stretches
each grey arc, airing the secret
unimaginable snows underneath.
But my friend is waving from the world's
far side. He, too, of the sea. O yes,
when we talk things slide off the table.

CLOCHARD

fallen pigeon, your red-rimmed eyes
and black claws give you away,
coat torn where the wings
broke off, face all gargoyled
by the sun's breath, whenever
it was you flew too high

Sunday, I think, on the Petit Pont,
the ledge barely wide enough
for your high-stepping dance
with three full turns, fan-tailed
as she braced for you, that brief
heraldic flare, her wink

the river tilting to glare
at your double skyward arc

PORTAIL DU CLOÎTRE

No lewdness or mirth, nor any
unchaste thoughts.
                    So far so good.
He blows dust from both faces,
inspects them for impurity.
O the anguish he'll carve out
of their sin round the corner
where noon slides over blank stone.
Facing him, but watching Eve,
his serpent spirals the tree
into woman. He considers
the spiteful twist of her glee
and finds it good. He knows women.
Look at that brazen nakedness
crowning the branches like fruit.

NIGHT IN THE ATELIER

for Tereska Levin

The borrowed key so easy
in the lock, you'd think it mine
this soul straying barefoot
from carved sleep. Faces
fix the space, absorbed,
lost in lost thoughts.
Nearly dawn and here I am
lusting for words. Or is it absence
– so intense the air is strung with it –
that's doing the talking?
Oils, bronze, wood
catch the dream, the dreamer gone.
And is there no translating
such a pact with stillness
beyond a bird's pi-*ti* pi-*ti*,
the swelling light as *Daphnis*
spins a sunrise, cellos
taking mutes off
one by one?

MARCHÉ

If he hears the caged panic

of quails ducks chickens
he gives no sign, crouched

slope-eared and childishly white
on the roof of the topmost hutch
not for escape

or suicide, but to show off
how plump; beware
his terrible softness
haunts the hand.

IN THE INTERVAL

between locking my door
and tapping at the surgeon's

a hag on a bench croons
to her cat, We'll never tell them

will we, chouchou? Hibiscus flowers
open wide, put out slender tongues.

A fading stare chalked on stone;
dung beetles' plated indifference.

Holding these against the light
for clues. – Just a game, really,

I tell the purple dress hanging
absently in a windowframe.

TRACKS

... then mid-sentence the train slowed
and stopped. What were we saying
and did it matter? Where are we?
The doors slide wide
on a field caught unawares.
Please do not leave until you're told.
We half-smile, foolish, dangling
from threads as the world spins on.
Some lean out into space and see
others leaning out, how the rails curve
and vanish both ways.

Why here? nobody's asking. Why now?
From all the journey this one instant
snagged. Sky lies puddled
in scattered constellations whose names
are secret. Secret, too, the reek
of urine from the tracks. *We who were here
and have gone.* Such things to ponder
so that when the 10.20 express screams past
there's quiet detachment in our looking on,
knowing fast trains for what they are,
heavy and light-headed with knowing.

Between these solemn rails and those,
a yellow carnival of groundsel dances
off along the gravel. Almost irresistible
the urge to jump. *If not now, when?*
Korczak's doomed children
clamber from the halted cattle cars

and frolic away through meadows,
as Wajda holds to the sweet betrayal
of happy endings.

            It was never meant
for treading, this *terra firma* suddenly sacred
and a long way down. But the word is given,
ladders produced. People and baggage
spill out to birdsong (another train
has sidled up).

            Perhaps a snake
likewise glances back at the skin it has shed.
Sees right through it. That winking translucence,
the verb *to be* receding through present perfect,
past simple, past perfect and then, where the track
arcs left, lost to view.

THE SECRET ART OF CLOUD DISPERSAL

for Gil, in memory of my father

This time the storm left its dead
high up. Among torn branches
lumbering our balcony
the woodpigeon almost at home.
Four droplets ride its back's
soft thunder; neat as a curtsey
the tucked wings, twig feet
head turned blind to one side.

They had found him almost sleeping
in a valley loud with long rains.
Still the mind slips on muddy slopes
into free fall. He taught us once
the secret art of cloud dispersal,
staring up at small summer ones
till they dissolved. It worked.
To conjure kindness from nothing,
reread Spinoza in a straw hat,
publish books where buried pain
pulses on. Burial isn't
the last word, is it.

       The tree
that framed a foreign childhood
turned up on this hill to drop
mulberries by the grave. No one
planted it; none pass here but birds.

DRIFT

Tap-end raised, the bow plunges
steeply sending up tall sprays
of grass, wild garlic, sorrel,
poppies, aslant on either side.
Rainwater held in the tilt
is greening, as if this wasteland
taken aboard in small doses
could one day be internalized,
exile less empty; maybe
creepers will grope through the two
sockets to anchor the drift,
and blown earth plug the hole's mute
protest. But now a bath
remains alone with itself,
nakedness having stepped out
a last time.

WADI SIAH

Black cypresses hold back the dead
where the gorge has sliced the ground
clean away. A winking of marble
behind linked branches: you're being
watched. This clumsy joy finding footholds
for a zigzag descent to the sea.
As if the air isn't already spiked
with the whiff of rains bound to come
thunderous down such cleavage.
On its mulchy floor a blackbird
flicks through tattered catalogues.

Three hundred and sixty-five steps
Old Khayyat built, tripping helter-skelter
down the ridge to the shore. An uphill or
a downhill year, he'd joke. Good humoured
the waves come lolloping falling
over themselves in the low sun.

A black-swathed figure.

　　　　　　　It happens. A cargo
half-forgotten in the hold, in its heaviness
shifts. Barely audible the words he'd finally found:
I'm not very good at it. – Life, I mean.
She seems to know, wading in, dark skirts
a widening ceremony; no sorrows beyond her.
If one splashed out to where she stands
would she take a child's hand and hold fast?

Or does it haunt the tongue for good, *the secret taste of being lost*? There's hammered gold dancing
a crazy path this way from the west.
The sky still open for late-comers.

NEOLITHIC

no night was ever this black

squatting in an ancestor's
skull with the smell of old terrors

toothed and sudden, their leap
carved on the mind's wall

that your fingers will retrace
until the slow florescence

of day on clefts and cobwebs,
and two high buzzards like motes

in a blue eye

APPRENTICESHIP

stepping onto night sands
or two heads afloat in the bay

whatever there was lived in
the silences between us

like a Himalayan bird
impossibly, the empty air

dizzy where two languages
not meeting forced unspoken words

to wing it above the drop
to find the voice – so familiar

now, it seems I invented you
for what you couldn't say

DIAPASON

Dry thistles
          barbed wire
to keep out revenants, their present tense,
the moist flesh-tinted apparition
these stones dream of.
    Back to the old symmetries.
What holds on, lets go, climbs
the masonry and stares in
slow as a stretch of late sun
    on the floortiles
where each tread's gritty rumination
echoes.
         How the blood
thuds in emptied air. It's time,
            pulling out all the stops
  playing deep chords on magnificent pipes
that plumb three floors from rafters to cellar.
    Too much for the ceilings. Effusive
they're unpeeling layers unthinkable
day in, day out, not to speak
of nights in these high-pitched rooms.
Two armchairs unbound
     sprawl in abandon
as one. How to figure whose silence
this is, talking out of a caperbush
      that leaps from the wainscot –

        ... love was not other than this: it groped
        silently among the things around us

to explain why we don't want to die
so passionately.

There are lines
taking shape before you know it
    on walls, lichen's oblique ramifications,
an infinitesimal tenderness
    finding patterns to survive by.
                        This being
the dry season, the unwatered figs
    we pick by the broken shed
have not yet mustered sweetness, just a faint
edenic fragrance. It will do.

GEOMANCY

Don't be fooled by the long
impassivity of roads –
    barricaded
    in the quiet hours
    they lay themselves
    impossibly open
    for the reckoning.
No mistaking the red cloth
flung off, looped
above the drop.
Rootfibres tense.
    Note how a bent
    nail still holds
    nothing together.

Or else the sheer
heave of what's been lost
    erupts – nightmares
    tossing and turning
    a side street, till it rolls
    over against the wall
    dragging the tarmac with it.
Now there's doubt underfoot.
Subsoil's gone awkwardly
public, rude with stones.
An intimacy squandered.
    But this is the way
    isn't it. So you said.
    One way or another.

FALLS

When you flung yourself over the edge
all daggers and frothing thunder

did you see how the old plane tree
below leans across deep silk breathing

long and slow? It takes five hundred years
to reach that kind of proficiency

inclining towards the unstoppable
dinning wall of water, to offer

for reflection a million leaves'
five-finger exercises in green

where the pitted surface heals
in quiet eddies, the pain receding.

ROBIN

for Michael Longley

It fell plumb
as an exclamation mark
à propos of nothing, onto the path

singularly
itself, drenched and hunched before me
by some errant providence

like the poet
long booked and bookmarked, chanced on
sodden outside the Festival Hall

'waiting for
a Polish fella', and a too-late
umbrella was all I could offer.

Though these hands
make a clumsy bower, Levant
rain and bird words skittering

on my lips,
the tiny midnight eyes unshutter
at last, curves adjust and I am branch

in the grip
of fantastical feet, a quickening
like that plumed penultimate line

lifting off.

NIJINSKY'S SHOES

The god of dance used to pick
flesh from his thumbs till they bled,
one hand playing eagle

to the other's Prometheus.
Steel-sprung the impulse
revolving him mid-air

triggered once on coming to
in a doss-house in Chelsea
(no Polish or Russian spoken)

when he flew in *grands jetés*
over twenty beds nonstop
by way of introduction.

Words came second anyway
hobbled by shyness or else
explosive. Safest in notebooks.

– St. Moritz, 1919: Danced
the madman for hotel guests
till God said, Enough. Then stopped.

Narcissus, never forewarned
in studio mirrors, lips parted
on the brink. And all the time

your mind making itself up
to take leave of your senses,
barefoot into the snowstorm.

TANGO

This is the exercise for this morning

how to dance
sitting down
               – CHARLES OLSON

To get it right, imagine you are
in italics: fleet, oblique
your parallel incline, one hand
in the small of her back – slant
thoughts exposed, sublimities
suddenly made yours sleekly
in saxophone curves.

Did he see, Aldus Manutius,
the way his cursive print would learn
to murmur in the ear, configured
intent and svelte as skaters
on the frozen canals behind San Marco?
A body-language insisting
there is more than meets the eye.

So. The passion is in the diagonal.
A slow tilting – that's it – to the edge
of control. Hold – two, three, four.
Feel the air resisting; it's the nothing
that will partner you always. It's how
a crow rampant against the wind beats
time then yields, folds, and is lifted away

glissando. You can also practise alone;
sometimes the mind slopes off by itself
heady with having a body. Work on
tangents, the unexpected stretch
sidelong. And listen for the pulse.
That's all. Now take my hand, my word.
Lean into the music.

DANCER, KEEP OUT

the fading sign nailed
to a gate, how could I
– back erect, feet in second
position – not take it
personally having just
that morning got the hang
of woodpigeons' jazzy
cuneiform patter on the rooftiles
over my head, no two sequences
the same (the maddening
secret of their improvisation)
as the dance compels
thought to catch its own shape,
the split-second flare of waves'
white underskirts before
the dying fall, the act
none can follow
even winged, even taut
with the excess of such music.
Only much later
does another reading
spring to mind: the dancer
isn't you at all but
splendidly alone
on the other side, honing
the forbidden perfection
of Degas' terracotta models,
each pose firmly

staked for balance
– that jarring, necessary line
the eye will disregard
preferring wonder.

NIGHT SONG

And so they go unsaid, those lines
drawn up in sleep – whole stanzas
galloping off in shapely masses
at dawn, the air left shaken.
Sometimes a phrase lingers
and lets itself be caught,
becoming strangely, shyly mine:
... till it rose from the page, donned nightfall
and turned in ... – A thing lost in thought,
deaf to me. So much for possession.
And whose was it anyway, that poem
reciting itself in your voice,
startled by my untimely waking?
... and the pure centrestep ... That's all,
but it sings, it sings, meaning
more than I can tell.

ARABIA OXEYE

for Gabriel Levin

April says it with yellow flowers.
Not just the niceties of milk-vetch,
mustard, love-in-a-mist, scabious.
I mean the quilled, laconic speech
of broom, how it utters each bloom
perfectly, pointedly, fragrance
exhaling the thought of it, like rhyme
adding a further peculiar sense.
I mean the way the desert springs surprise:
gold hawkbit, fleabane, vipergrass;
and this Arabia oxeye
I offer you – knocked sideways
by your latest from the wilderness,
tinctures pressed from words to voice the eye.

CISTERN REVISITED

come the winter rains
old claims run deep
and fast down alleys
in the Valley of Spirits

storming stone courtyards
in muscled torrents
to swerve converge grey-
brown from three sides then

wrestle the sluice-gate
you'd meant as a window
for daylight squinting down
on books pooled high enough

to float a poet year round,
or wet his lips to speak
the desert in its voices,
or slake the thirst of friends

who find you waist-deep mildly
fishing for others to add
to the French, Greek, Arabic
writers pegged rakish to dry

I'D LIKE TO SUBMIT THIS CAMEL

Mine is the rumped arabesque swagger
up sheer paths, hips and teats a slow blues
number, with syncopated chewing
on jut-toothed jaws. O take me I'm yours.

I can fold down to sphinx like a poem
haunting your pocket, night in my eyes,
sweet-milked always from closing my lips
on acacia thorns. O take me I'm yours,

and my feet will tattoo the desert
with galloping scansion, tread bright air
like Buraq off the face of the earth.
Saddled with words. O take me I'm yours.

Buraq: in Islamic tradition, the winged steed on which
the Prophet Mohammad rose to heaven.